The Diary of
BENJAMIN CARPENTER
Tanks Corps

Edited by Christine Considine

Benjamin Carpenter
Queens Westminster Rifles regiment

To my father Dennis J Carpenter for keeping the diary safe and passing it on.

To Antoine Berthe for showing me where it all happened and really bringing the diary to life.

Introduction

THIS IS A transcription of the pocket diary of Benjamin Colin Carpenter, my paternal grand-father.

I have kept the spellings, abbreviations and punctuation as in the original (assuming I have read his beautiful handwriting correctly). He appears to have been a fan of the semi-colon, but not the apostrophe.

The layout is also the same, so it does jump about a bit when an entry takes up more than the 5 lines per day allowed. It is a week to two pages, starting on a Sunday, with a Mem (Memorandum) as the last item each week.

It is mainly written in pencil, apart from a few weeks in April and May when it is written in purple ink.

Diary

The diary itself is a black leather bound Charles Letts Self Opening Diary, number 30, for 1919. It measures 9.5cm x 5.5cm with colour pictures of decorations (ribbons) awarded for Honourable service on inside of front cover, and a black and white map of The Great War Western Front on inside of back cover. Just in case you were diary geeks!

Benjamin Carpenter

Born in Camberwell on 4th September, 1883 to Benjamin Samuel and Jane Pullinger. Eldest of three sons.

Maternal grandfather was Colin Pullinger of Selsey, Sussex, inventor of the Pullinger Perpetual Mouse-Trap in 1860. By 1885 over two million sold. Factory employed 40 people and was biggest employer in Selsey and made 960 a week.

Paternal grandfather was Benjamin Samuel Carpenter of Lambeth, a Rocking Horse maker.

Pre-war occupation: Insurance Clerk

Enlisted in 1916 into the London Regiment, Queen's Westminster Rifles at the age of 32.

Was 5'2" and ¾" tall.

Joined Tank Corps at Central Workshops on 26th January, 1917.

Transferred to Army Reserves on demobilization 22nd November, 19.

Presumably served as Tank Crew, not just in

office at CWS, as photograph shows Tank Crew badge on his sleeve.

Also must have served in Machine Gun Corps as photo of him in uniform with MGC cap badge. War records listed as 'burnt documents' at The National Archives.

Married at Camberwell Register Office to Elsie Maud Egan 30th May, 1919 younger daughter of Arthur Egan and Mary Ann Long. Two sons Geoffrey and Dennis

Post war occupation: Insurance Clerk

Older son Geoffrey served in RAF Died in crash of Dakota KN630 25th August, 1950 in Malaysia.

Reburied at Cheras Road CWGC Cemetery 15th March, 2012, along with all crew members with full Military honours. Attended by Dad and myself.

Benjamin Carpenter died in 1974 age 91, leaving his widow, son, daughter-in-law and three granddaughters.

Benjamin Carpenter
Machine Gun Corps.

Benjamin Carpenter
1883 to 1974

1 Wednesday

2 Thursday

3 Friday

More rain. In evg to C.C Farm for washing &
Supper hut. Weather mild. Rations very poor.
No marge for days.

4 Saturday

Rain again. Wrote letters in afternoon. Dinner
with Billy, Jimmy & AOC boys etc. at Cafe de
la Gare Blangy. Had a good time.

Mem

Extension till 10 o'c at Cafe. Lorry took us from
Stores & brought us back. Dinner at 6.30. Sing
song afterwards.

5 Sunday

Took it easy morn & afternoon. To Supper hut & Blangy in evg. A miserable morn & afternoon. Much rain but cleared in evg.

6 Monday

A finer day. Some sunshine. With Burns, Perkins & Barrington to Farm for supper & afterwards to T. Cappelle.

7 Tuesday

No rain today. To Supper Hut & Erin. Started "Refresher Courses" a few days ago for men from the line.

8 Wednesday

A fine day. Mild & sunny. Afternoon off. Had a good walk in afternoon through Blangy towards Bealencourt. Back to Camp about 6 & then to Florries for supper with Bradbury & party. A good evg.

9 Thursday

Lot of rain early morning. Cleared up later. To Blangy in evg. Met Hinton. Red tape & discipline in Camp being made sterner.

10 Friday

No rain & fairly bright. To Erin & C.C in evg. Met Masons. Am still in best of health & spirits

11 Saturday

A wet afternoon. Stayed in & wrote letters. To C.C in evg. Rations a little better but still not enough to eat.

12 Sunday

No rain but overcast. Dodged Ch. Parade as usual. Directly after dinner with Knot to Abercourt & Maisoncelle. Back at midnight.

13 Monday

About a week ago a large number of men came down the line for a Refresher Course. There was nothing much for them to do; they got fed up

& dissatisfied & asked to be sent back but were refused. They struck work today. In evening to Anvin on way back met Joe Clarke. No rain today.

14 Tuesday

General down soon after 8 to address the strikers, he said a few words to us as well. "Strikers" to go back to their Units. No rain but very dull. To Blangy in evg.

15 Wednesday

More rain again today. To farm for washing in afternoon & then bath. To C.Canteen in evg. Met Mason.

16 Thursday

A nice bright mild day, but some rain in evg. To 3rd Advcd Wks in morn. To Erin in evg.

17 Friday

Master on leave again. Another fine bright day. To 3rd Adv in morn & Erin in evg. Has turned cold.

18 Saturday

Fine day, no rain. Have a bad cold. To Erin in evg

19 Sunday

Cold but fine. Stayed in until the evg owing to cold, & then to Supper Hut & Suzannes

20 Monday

A fine bright morn but cold. My cold a trifle better. To 3rd Adv in morn & C.C in evg

Brad. demob

21 Tuesday

A beautiful bright cold day. To Blangy in evg with Mason. Cold much better. A few men going home for demob every day now. Ten today.

22 Wednesday

A lovely bright cold day.. To Bergonoise in afternoon. Dance in Camouflage Hanger in evg. Not bad.

23 Thursday

Another bright cold day. To C.C & Anvin in evg. Met Langley, Roberts etc . Cold nearly well. A very cold night.

24 Friday

Still very cold. To Erin in evg. Another bed burnt.

25 Saturday

Cold & dull. Wrote letter in afternoon. To Supper hut in evg. C.C. closes tonight. Opening at Supper Hut.

Mem

Our people doing everything they can to keep men & persuading them to stop over.

26 Sunday

To Hesdin with Burns & Lockley. Caught train at Blangy soon after 10 & returned by train about 6pm. Had a good time. Weather very cold but bright. Fall of snow during night & more during day. Finished up at Blangy.

27 Monday

Weather very wintry. More snow & also sunshine. In evg to Farm for washing & then to Erin. Met Mason. Worked a bit late.

28 Tuesday

Another bright cold day. Snow still on ground. To 3rd Adv Wks in morn as usual. Went back after tea & then to Farm with washing & after that to S.hut

29 Wednesday

Left camp for Bapaume. Got a lift Ford Box Anvin to Wavrans. Saw Charlie H. Stayed with him the night. Out in evg with C & Jock

30 Thursday

Weather still cold & dull today. Left Camp about 10. C. came with me to St Pol. Had a lift in lorry. Dinner at St P. Left about 1. Picked up by Box car. Arrived Arras soon after 2.30. Had a look around. Spent a long time finding rest Camp. To theatre in evg. A concert party on – good. Back to billet. A very cold night.

31 Friday

Cold & dull. Visited old dug out in Com trench in front of Anzin where I slept when first went up the line. Left Arras about 2. Walked nearly all the way to Bapaume . Slept in caravan attached to steam roller. Tired out & feet sore.

1 Saturday

Push on to Courcelette. Get a lift part of the way. Cannot find dear old Dode's grave. Stop at Canadian Camp for the night. They make me very comfy.

2 Sunday

Have another search for grave. Did not find it. Leave Courcelette about 1. Reach Amiens about 9.30. Got lift part of the way to Albert. After leaving A. & walking 4 or 5 miles a Frenchman gave me a lift in his horse drawn van. Many stops at Cafes. An adventurous ride & very cold. Stop at Rest Camp. A horrible place. No blankets. Very cold.

3 Monday

Have a rough breakfast at rest camp & another one at an Hotel where I engage a room. Have a good look round the town & see a Concert Party at the theatre in the evg. Early to bed.

4 Tuesday

Another look round town. Leave by 12.12 for St Pol. Arrive soon after 6!! Have a feed then walk to Driving Camp. Stay there the night.

5 Wednesday

Spent morn in hut except to go to Farm for coffee with Erb & co. Left C soon after dinner. Rode all the way to C.W. by lorry. More snow today.

6 Thursday

Feel out of sorts & have a cold. Snow fairly deep. Bright sunshine & thaw during day. To supper hut in evg. Met Mason, Jock etc. Mason off on 1 mos leave tomorrow.

7 Friday

A <u>very</u> cold day. Keen E wind. To supper hut in evg. Still feel off colour. Porridge & <u>fried cheese</u> for breakfast.

8 Saturday

Awfully cold day. Still unwell. Stomach out of order. Did not leave camp. Spent most of time in Rec hut writing letters.

9 Sunday

Still very cold. Stayed in bed until tea time. Bad pains in stomach & diah. Wrote letters in Rec Hut in evg.

10 Monday

Bright sunshine all day. A slight thaw at mid-day. A very cold night. Spent evg in Rec Hut writing letters & playing chess with Lockley.

11 Tuesday

Brilliant sunshine again today but still awfully cold. Once more feel myself again. To Blangy in evg. Meet Sgt Jarvis

12 Wednesday

Blue sky & brilliant sunshine but very cold. Wrote letters in afternoon, to Supper Hut in evg. Very disappointed over demob.

13 Thursday

Blue sky & sunshine. Not so cold in evg. To Farm for washing & then to Odells. Having another attack of indigestion.

14 Friday

Much milder. Thaw during day. Told on parade no more men would be released until 80 tanks had been repaired. They estimate the time at 2 mos. To Blangy in evg.

15 Saturday

Thaw continues. Temp has been nearly down to zero. Stop in camp all day. Hold meetings regarding our retention. Wrote letters in evg.

16 Sunday

Left soon after 9 for Fruges with Lockley. There by Foden back by train. Rather rainy day. Played billiards in afternoon. Stopped at Berguenese for evg.

17 Monday

A very mild day. Frightfully muddy. Have another cold & feel off colour. Spent evg in Rec Room writing.

18 Tuesday

Mild & wet. To Dance in evg & then to Odells. Not much doing in Works.

19 Wednesday

Afternoon off as usual. Wrote letters also in evg & then down to supper hut. Met Whiteley & ?Cobler
Mild & wet.

20 Thursday

A pleasant mild morn & mild later. Again wrote letters in evg & then down to Supper Hut. Bread ration for sometime past, very good, but we still get too much bully.

21 Friday

A mild & bright morn, but heavy rain all afternoon & evg. In evg to Rec Hut & then Supper Hut. Still have cold otherwise feel fit.

22 Saturday

Still mild & wet. Wrote letters in afternoon. Saw our Panto in the evg. Not bad.

Mem

In order a few days ago "Fuel 20lbs per hut per day <u>when available</u>" Some ration!! We in our hut looking after ourselves very well though.

23 Sunday

Rissoles for breakfast. Cold bully for dinner. To Auchy in afternoon. Our footballers there. Tea at ASC camp. Got back by lorry to Blangy where York & I dropped off. On J.B in late by back way

24 Monday

Still mild & wet. In Supper Hut in evg & then to Odells. Met Billy.

25 Tuesday

No change in weather. Generally have a little sunshine during the day. My cold still. To Odelles in evg.

26 Wednesday

In Rec Hut writing in afternoon. ~~French~~ All drinks still v.dear & weak.

27 Thursday

Dull & overcast. To 3rd Adv in morn. Came up for tea at 4.30.

28 Friday

Still very mild. To supper hut in evg. Met Pick-up & Harry Barber

Mem 23 SUND

Heard a lark singing for the first time this year. Other birds are also sounding a few notes. There is already a feeling of Spring in the air.

1 Saturday

A fine bright day. Wrote letters in afternoon. To Blangy in evg.

2 Sunday

A fine Springlike day after rain in early morn. To Fruges at 9.30 with Billy Whiteley by train from Anvin. Tea at Berguenuese.

3 Monday

Raining all day. Spent evg in Rec Hut writing letters. Weather v.mild. Two of our men have lately died from Flu.

4 Tuesday- Shrove Tuesday

Another wet day but cleared in evg. To Blangy. A Carnival. Boys in masks & costumes!!

5 Wednesday

Dull in morn but afternoon bright & fine & Springlike. After dinner to Farm for washing. Wrote letters & later on in evg to Supper Hut.

6 Thursday

Strong N.E gale with heavy rain early morn. Rained throughout day until early evg. To supper hut after dance.

7 Friday

Another very dull & wet day. To supper hut in evg. A spirit of unrest in Camp again. Use of dining hall to hold meeting denied us.

8 Saturday

Dull, mild & showery. Took washing to Farm in evg& then went to Supper Hut. Where do the profits from the suppers go?

9 Sunday

Fine during day but misty rain in evg. Wrote letters in afternoon & to Blangy in evg.

10 Monday

Still dull & wet. Writing letters first part of evg & then to Amys. Bread rations very short.

11 Tuesday

A fine day, no rain & brighter. In evg letter writing & then to Erin. To 3rd Adv in morning.

12 Wednesday

A bright day; no rain. Russian draft moved to Stores. Played cards all afternoon. To Blangy in evg. Met Horner.

13 Thursday

A bright & windy day. The ground drying up beautifully. Went up to tea at 4.30. To dance in evg & then to Odelles.

14 Friday

More rain again & colder. Left off raining in evg. To Erin. Met Langley & Roberts in Olgas

15 Saturday

Played cards from after dinner until lights out.

16 Sunday

Mild showery & bright intervals. Went to Stores to see Russian draft off. To Anvin in evg.

17 Monday

Some rain. Some sunshine. To Pictures in evg first time since they have moved to our camp & then to Supper Hut.

18 Tuesday

Stormy in morn, finer by afternoon. Dance in Camouflage in evg. Somerville my partner. After to Supper Hut.

19 Wednesday

Played cards in afternoon. To Blangy in evg. Sleet on my way home.

20 Thursday

Woke up to find it snowing hard also windy & cold. Cleared up before Dinner time. Afternoon bright & fine. Wrote letters & then to supper hut.

21 Friday

A cold, bleak dull day. In evg to dance at F Batts Camp at Blangy. Not at all exciting. Reached home about 11.30 !!

22 Saturday

Still dull.* Played cards all the afternoon. Wrote letters for a short time in evg & then to supper hut.

*Brighter afternoon.

23 Sunday

A bright fine day but rather cold. At cards all afternoon. Writing letters in evg & then to supper hut.

24 Monday

A little snow this morn & a pretty keen E wind. Wrote letters in evg & then went to Odelles. A cold night.

25 Tuesday

Cold & dull a cutting E. wind. To dance in evg & then to Erin. Not a bad dance this time. More trouble over men taking their tea from ?mess room.

26 Wednesday

Played cards all the afternoon. Letter writing in evg & then to Canteen. Met Jock Kent & others there. Jock K being demobbed tomorrow. After leaving Canteen went down to Odelles.

27 Thursday

Heavy showers & cold S.W. wind. To supper hut in evg. After my return played cards until nearly midnight.

28 Friday

A cold wind & very dull. Feel a little slack. Did not go out but played cards the whole evg.

29 Saturday

Heavy snow in morn. Cleared up before dinner & afterwards brilliant sunshine rest of day. Wrote letters played cards & to supper hut.

30 Sunday

A very bright day but cold. One or two short snow storms. Wrote letters, played cards & went down to supper hut.

31 Monday

Cold & bright. To Blangy in evg with Liptrot. Left washing at Farm on way.

1 Tuesday

Awoke to find another heavy fall of snow on ground. Turned much warmer in afternoon, sun came out & snow disappeared. To dance in evg & then supper hut.

2 Wednesday

Misty morn, but fine & bright for rest of day. Resting & writing in afternoon. In evg to Teneur & T.Capelle then to supper hut.

3 Thursday

A lovely bright day but a bit cold. Feel a little off colour. In evg to Teneur, T.Capelle & supper hut. Met Billy W.

4 Friday

Another fine bright day. Rather cold first thing, hard frost in night. To Blangy in evg.

5 Saturday

Fine again & a little milder. Feel a trifle off colour. Read & slept in afternoon. For a short time to dance in evg & then to supper hut.

Mem

No wood in camp two days this week. We managed all right though.

6 Sunday

A fine, mild spring day. Left Camp about 9 for Fruges, also visited Verchon, Berguinose & Heuchin. Returned to Camp about 11.

7 Monday

Another fine day. To supper hut in evg. Still feel slightly off colour.

8 Tuesday

Weather still fine mild & bright. To dance in evg & afterwards to supper hut.

9 Wednesday

Another fine day. Read & slept in afternoon. To Blangy in evg. Met Cpl Clark. Do not feel quite myself yet.

10 Thursday

Dull & wet. In evg wrote letter & then to supper hut.

11 Friday

Dull with a strong S.W. wind & a fair quantity of rain. Feel much more myself. To supper hut in evg.

12 Saturday

Letter writing in afternoon. A party of W.A.A.C.S. from Aberville in Camp. Dance in evg. Not bad. Saw two pals home to Chateau. A fine day.

Mem

Three lorries with troops ran from our place to Abbeville on Easter Monday. The men had a good time. About half a dozen left behind & returned next day.

13 Sunday

Dull morn, beautiful afternoon & evg. Took it easy in afternoon. After tea to Maisoncelle with Griffiths. Had a good time. Home about 3am!!!

14 Monday

A bad day, strong S.W. wind & heavy rains. Did not feel at all well. To supper hut in evg with Liptrot.

15 Tuesday

Strong S.W. wind & heavy showers again. To dance & then to supper hut. Met the two Bills there. I feel much better.

16 Wednesday

Still strong winds & heavy rain. Took it easy in afternoon. In evg to Pictures & then to supper hut.

17 Thursday

Gale over & no rain but very overcast. Wrote letter evg & then to supper hut. Felt in normal health & spirits.

18 Friday – Good Friday

No holiday. Toasted cheese & bread for break-fast only. Fine but dull. In evg wrote letter & then to supper hut. Met the two Billys.

19 Saturday

Bright, but chilly wind. To Farm for washing in afternoon. To supper hut in evg. Am feeling A 1 again.

Mem

Doors of cinema locked five mins before end of show & opened after G. save the King had been sung.

20 Sunday – Easter Day

Bright & fine but a nippy E. wind. Left Camp soon after 9 with J.Clark for Berck Plage. Reached there soon after 3. To beach, up light-house & cafes in evg.

21 Monday

Up about 7.30. Had a good breakfast &
had a walk inland. Caught 4.30 train to
Montroix then a fast goods to Anvin. Reached
A about 7.30 then to supper hut & home by
9.30. Weather same as yesterday. Had a very
enjoyable trip but weather rather cold.

22 Tuesday

Still bright with a cold E. wind. To dance in
evg & then supper hut with Liptrot. A very fine
sun set.

23 Wednesday

Wrote letters in afternoon. In evg to Farm for
washing & then to supper hut with Liptrot. A
trifle milder but overcast.

24 Thursday

Still dull & chilly. In evg to supper hut &
Odellls with Liptrot & Fleetwood. Feel in best
of health & spirits. Had some roast mutton this
week & not so many stews.

25 Friday

*Overcast & cold. To Farm, supper hut &
Odells in evg with Liptrot. Am fed up with the
bad weather.*

26 Saturday

*Heavy showers during the day with some
bright intervals. In afternoon with Snow to
Heuchin. Caught 6.20 train to Fruges & had
to walk all the way home. Got pretty wet.*

27 Sunday

*A fairly fine morn, but much rain after dinner.
Wrote letters in afternoon & part of evg & then
to supper hut & afterwards Odells. Had jolly
time.*

28 Monday

*Awoke to find a heavy fall of snow on ground
& still snowing hard. Had continuous showers of snow, hail & sleet right up to middle of
afternoon. To S. Hut.*

29 Tuesday

*A very wet chilly day. Do not feel at all well.
We are getting powdered milk. Again stayed in
in evg & played cards.*

30 Wednesday

*Another wet windy cold day. Writing in after-
noon. To Blangy in evg with Joe Clark*

*Postcard showing the lighthouse and
maritime hospital at Berck Plage*

1 Thursday

A finer day. Weather seems to be on the change for the better. Clothing Parade. New Tunic, Slacks & Putties. To Blangy in evg to have clothes altered.

2 Friday

Return to old conditions. Wet & dismal. Pay parade at 4.30. At night a noisy hut; a sing song.

3 Saturday

Misty morning, fine afternoon & evg. Waacs from Maresquel down for a dance. Had a good time.

4 Sunday

Heard cuckoo for first time this year & also frogs croaking in evg on our way home. A layer of mist on ground looked ????? Much warmer. Misty in morn, a lovely afternoon & evg. To Auchy by back road with Clarke. Home about 11.30. Had a good outing.

5 Monday

At last a fine warm summerlike day. In evg called at Stores & then to supper hut.

6 Tuesday

Another beautiful day. To usual dance in evg. Quite good. After to supper hut & cafes in Erin. Got in late

7 Wednesday

A very fine day. To Maresquel in afternoon on bicycle. Met Thompson there. Had tea & set off for Auchy. Had a steak & a chips at Hesdin. Found I had a puncture. Had a row with a Major. Finished up about 1am at Blanches. Very jolly there. Remainder of Batt being demobbed.

8 Thursday

Another lovely day. In evg with Joe Clarke to Blangy & towards Bealancourt. Met J. A fine night home about 11pm

9 Friday

*A very warm fine day. Wrote letters in evg
& then to supper hut & Odells. French leave
stopped & ordinary leave slowed down owing
to task not being completed.*

10 Saturday

*Another lovely day. Writing & reading in
afternoon & then to supper hut. A sharp short
thunderstorm in afternoon*

11 Sunday   £29

*A lovely day, very hot. A sharp short thunder-
storm in afternoon. After tea to Maisoncelles
with Joe. A lovely evg. Home about 12.30*

12 Monday

*Overcast & rain in morn ; cleared up a fine
afternoon & evg. Machoniche for breakfast,
stew for dinner & cheese for tea. To supper hut
in evg.*

13 Tuesday

Lovely weather again. In evg to our Canteen & then to Olga's with Joe Roberts Ginger C & Tom Langley

14 Wednesday

Another grand day. A party of Waacs to Camp. Dance in evg. Down to Erin after.

15 Thursday

A beautifully fine hot morn, but overcast & cooler in afternoon. Wind changed from S.E to S.W. Had a swim this morn about 11 with Joe thoroughly enjoyed it. In evg to Blangy with Joe

16 Friday

A lovely day. In morn another swim in river with Joe. To Olga's etc in evg & finished off at 3rd Adv with Shaw, Joe, Tom, & Ginger

17 Saturday

Weather perfect. Saw last tank go down to Stores & then off to Hesdin. Met Taffy Davis at Auchy. Walked all the way to H & slept at village just outside in a barn with 2 French soldiers. They were good pals.

18 Sunday

Set off for Abbeville. Had not walked very far when French civvy car picked me up. Had good walk round A. & left about 4. Got home by jumping lorries. One lorry I rode in conveying party of R.A.F.s back to Maresquel.. Had a good outing.

19 Monday

Grand weather. Took it easy until evg & then to Odells, Olgas etc with boys. Finished up late at Florries. A good time. Girls in tears.

20 Tuesday

Weather still lovely. Did not go to work, but went down to Blangy Stn & saw boys off. Stayed in in afternoon. Camp frightenly dull & quiet in evg. To S.Hut.

21 Wednesday

Weather unchanged. Just looked in at Office but did not do a stroke. Took it easy in afternoon. In evg to Stores dance. R.A.F. there.

22 Thursday

Another very fine day. Took it easy; just looked in at Works & thats all. To Blangy in evg.

23 Friday

Weather unchanged. Shirked work in morn. Looked in in afternoon but nothing to do. To Odells in evg.

24 Saturday

A grand day. Warned for leave!! To Maisoncelle to try & arrange a flight to Blighty then to Blangy for tunic. To dance in evg.

25 Sunday

Still very fine. Left Camp about 9 for Maisoncelle with John. No luck. Spent afternoon & evg in village. Slept at Aerodrome.

26 Monday

Misty first thing in morn – fine afterwards.
Set off for Blighty in airplane about 2 o/c
& reached Folkestone in about 35 mins. A
grand experience. Rather misty over Channel.
Arrived Vic. 7. Call at Es & get home about

27 Tuesday

Another fine day. Start out about 11. Lunch at
L.Corner Ho. Home again 4:30. Stayed in in
evg. E. came up about 8 o'c

28 Wednesday

Still fine. Saw Passmore in morn. Called at E's.
Saw P.C. in afternoon & then met C & V at
Bank. To Mays in evg with E.

29 Thursday

Still lovely weather. Called upon E about 12.
Up to West End for rings. Back to "62" very
tired.

30 Friday

A lovely day. M at 10.30. Left Pad. by 1:45 for Torquay, arrvd there at 6:45. Secured good digs without much difficulty.

31 Saturday

Lovely weather again. E & I bathed in morn. Took it easy in afternoon. Towards Babbacombe in evg. Got lost.

Benjamin and Elsie Carpenter on honeymoon, 6th June, 1919
Photo: Dinham & Sons, Torquay

1 Sunday   £20

Still perfect weather. E & I bathe at Bab in morn. In afternoon to Ansty Cove. To Paignton in evg

2 Monday

Weather perfect. I bathed in morn. Had a row in afternoon. To dance in evg.

3 Tuesday

Weather lovely. I bathe in morn. Row in afternoon. Leave boat in Daddy Holes Corner. To Theatre in evg.

4 Wednesday

A few spots of rain in morn. Lovely aft & evg. Took it easy in aft. To dance in evg.

5 Thursday

Weather fine but slightly overcast. All day trip to Plymouth by motor, via the moors. A grand ride.

6 Friday

*Still very fine & hot. Took it easy in morn.
Had photo taken in aft. To Paignton in evg.*

7 Saturday

*Weather unchanged. Caught the 11:45 to Pad.
Reached there about 4:30. Arrived with E at
62 about 7*

Mem

Both E & I weigh 8stn. 8lbs, June '19

8 Sunday

*Still fine. Stayed in all day. H called. Left for
Vic Stn soon after 11p.m. Slept at Y.M.*

9 Monday

*Fine, but overcast part of day. Left Vic at 6.30,
arrived Calais soon after 12. Left rest camp
soon after tea & went down into Town.*

10 Tuesday

A very fine hot day. Left Camp just before 9. Train started about 10.30. Reached Anvin via St Omer about 4p.m

11 Wednesday

Still fine & hot. Swung the lead in the morn. Holiday in afternoon. To Anvin evg. Rations poor.

12 Thursday

Still fine but v.strong S.W. wind. To Canteen in evg. Did not go out of Camp.

13 Friday

End of gale. Beautiful weather again. To Erin in evg.

14 Saturday

A lovely day. In evg with Ranns to Blangy. Had a good evg. Home late.

Mem

Church parades are now washed out. They are trying to put the screw on us again i.e belts, putties etc

15 Sunday

Awfully hot. Took it easy until after tea then had walk round Teneur. Finished up at Odells.

16 Monday

Weather unaltered. To Heuchin in evg with Titmus. Girl in cart drove us back as far as Anvin. Home late.

17 Tuesday

Still fine & very hot. Am doing very little work. To Erin in evg. Rations awful.

18 Wednesday

No change in weather. To Maisoncelle in evg. Home rather late. Had a slight touch of neuralgia lately.

19 Thursday

Still fine. To Stores Camp in evg. Met Harry &
others. Rain very badly needed.

20 Friday

Weather on the change. Had a little rain at
last. Biscuits for tea!! To Stores Camp in evg &
then with Harry & others to Tilly Capelle.

21 Saturday

A little rain in night but weather still quite
fine. In evg to Tilly Capelle with Horner &
Pickup.

Mem

Heard unofficially that Peace was signed. 28th
Sat

22 Sunday

Weather still fine. After dinner to Abricourt &
then on to Crepy. Met Jones & Garrish there.
Dancing. Left about 9 & then went to Florries.

23 Monday

Weather fine but cooler. To Odell's in evg. Met long Harry there. Feel a bit fed up.

24 Tuesday

Weather rather overcast, cool & some light showers. Early in the morn guard told us Peace had been signed. Wrote letters in morn. Called at Stores & saw Taffy Davis in afternoon & had a walk with him round Tilly Capelle. P.T.O.

25 Wednesday

Weather same as yesterday. Work in morn as usual. Had a nap in afternoon. To Stores Camp in evg. Met Harry.

26 Thursday

Weather overcast & chilly. Did not go out of Camp in evg. Feel rather fed up.

27 Friday

Fine, bright & warmer again. To Stores Camp in evg to see Taffy Davis. Had a walk round Teneur. Have a touch of neuralgia.

28 Saturday

Cool, overcast & some rain. After tea with Ranns, & Swift to Blangy, Bealancourt & home via Maisoncelle. Got in very late. (See Mem on prev page)

29 Sunday

A fairly fine day – some showers. Played cards in morn. To Crepy in afternoon with Davis. Called at Florries on way back.

30 Monday

Same type of weather. Only knew for certain today that Peace had been signed. To Canteen in evg & then cards until 12p.m

1 Tuesday

Cold & showery. Went to Farm in morning for washing. Did not go out in evg. played cards.

2 Wednesday

Overcast & showery. A party of the 7th Dragoons (French) visited our Camp for a football match, tea & to Cinema afterwards. We won 2-1

£28:10:0   £22

3 Thursday

Weather still un settled. Did not go out of Camp in evg. To Canteen. Feel a bit fed up.

4 Friday

Overcast & showery. Finished midday until Mond morn. Our Peace holiday. A special dinner. Soup, fish, rasin duff, cigar, cigarettes, cherries & a bottle of beer (over

Cont 24th June

Back to Camp for tea & then to Blangy with Ranns. Left Blangy about 2a.m Finished up in Madame Denis'

5 Saturday

Dull but warm. To Berck-Plage with Ranns. Passes did not come through. By time we had got pass too late (over

6 Sunday

Warm but very dull. Beach in morning. Afternoon in Town. Box car to Etaples. Soon afterwards Englishman with own car took us to Hesdin. Walked home from there. Arrived about 12. Very tired. Had a good time on the whole.

7 Monday

Weather still dull. Feel rather tired today. Did not go out of Camp.

8 Tuesday

Weather very dull, but not chilly. To Stores Camp in in evg. Called on Taffy. He was out. Back to our Canteen.

9 Wednesday

Dull in morning, fine & bright in afternoon. To Stores Camp in evg. Met Taffy. Neuralgia better.

10 Thursday

A lovely day; hot & bright. To Blangy in evg. Returned on Water Carrier with 2Lt Noon & Paddy. Stopped at Odells on way back.

11 Friday

Weather not so fine overcast. Did not go out of Camp in evg Feel rather fed up.

12 Saturday

Fine morn, very showery in afternoon & evg. Read during afternoon to Canteen in evg with Vaughn.

~~Mem~~

4th Fri *Called on Taffy Davis at Stores in afternoon. Did not go out of Camp in evg. Had a sing song in Canteen*

13 Sunday

Overcast & very frequent showers of heavy rain. Moped around in morn. Pontoon in afternoon. To Cinema in evg.

14 Monday

Another very showery dull day. Holiday on account of French Peace Celebrations. Did not go out of Camp until late in evg. & only as far as Odells

15 Tuesday

Still overcast & showery. To Mill with Taffy in evg. & afterwards to Odell. No pass no puttees. Police came into cafe late but all was serene.

16 Wednesday

A lovely day – hot. In afternoon to Maisoncelle & then across to Heuchin. Have now a 11 o'c pass

17 Thursday

Fine & hot again. In evg to Stores Camp for cigarettes soap etc then to Farm for washing. Back in camp about 8. Did not go out after.

18 Friday

Another fine day. In evg to Farm with washing & then to Stores Camp (Saw Dick) for cigarettes etc as am starting for Cologne tomorrow

19 Saturday

Fine but overcast. Left Blangy by 10:15. Changed at Etaples & arrvd Boulogne about 2. Had a look round the Town & left by 10pm train for Cologne.

5th Saturday to catch train . by "goods" to Hesdin & then 7.30 train to Etaples. Walked over bridge when Frenchman with cart picked us up & took us to B.P. Arrived 10:30

20 Sunday

Weather fine & brighter. Arrvd Cologne at 4 p.m. Had a good journey (sleeping bunck) on what was once a Hospital train the Adriatic. After fixing up at Leave Club had a look around the City.

21 Monday

A fine day but not very bright. Went into Cathedral, Museum & Council House. Tram ride in evg & then to Cafes. Much animation in streets.

22 Tuesday

Rained practically all day. In morn towards Zoo. Afternoon "Pictures" . evg to Music Hall –good.

23 Wednesday

Rained nearly all day. Left about 9 for motor trip. Went as far as Overath. Back at 4. To Crystal Palace in evg. good

24 Thursday

Band on board. Very fine scenery on Rhine. A very overcast day. Left about 9 for trip up the Rhine. By tram as far as Bohn. Went as far as Andernash. Returned by steamer to Coln. Cafes in evg

25 Friday

Dull but fine. To Zoo in afternoon & music hall in evg. have a very bad cold.

26 Saturday

Still very overcast. Round about the town all day. To cafes in evg. Cold still bad.

27 Sunday

Overcast & a few slight showers. To station in morn to enquire about train etc. Rested in afternoon. To Princess Cafe in evg. Left by 10:23

28 Monday

Weather still very overcast. Travelled by train "Grabrul". Arrived Calais 12:15. Caught 3:18 (narrow gauge train) to Fruges. Arrived about 8:30. Walked from F to Camp. Got home about 1 a.m

29 Tuesday

Still dull. To farm in morn. Slept in afternoon. In evg to Anvin with Ranns & then to Florries.

30 Wednesday

Still very dull. Had a sleep in afternoon. To Monchy Caioux to Waacs concert. A very poor show.

31 Thursday

Dull morning, but fine bright afternoon & evg. Feel off colour. Have not been out of Camp. To Canteen in evg with Vaughn.

3 — **Blangy-sur-Ternoise** - La Gare

Postcard showing the station at Blangy-sur-Ternoise

1 Friday

*Another dull day. In evg with Ranns to
Blangy. Back about 11.*

2 Saturday

*Still dull. Stayed in & read during afternoon.
Went to dance in evg. Waacs up from Monchy
Caioux. Not a bad time.*

3 Sunday

*A fine day – sunshine at last. To Paris-Plage.
Caught train at Anvin 10:15. Along beach in
afternoon. To dance Halls etc in evg. Met K.
stayed at Hotel da la Gare.*

4 Monday

*Fine again today. Along front in morn. Left
P.P. at 2:30. Arrvd Anvin about 5:30 where
we spent evg. With Peploe & his pal*

5 Tuesday

*Dull once more. Out with Ranns in evg. To
Erin & Anvin. Dance in cafe in latter place.*

6 Wednesday

A brighter day. Read during afternoon. To Maisoncelle in evg. A fine evg. Feel much better.

~~£29~~   ~~£26~~   £16-9-0

7 Thursday

Dull again. Did not go out of Camp. Played Housey in Canteen & then Coblers hut.

8 Friday

A beautiful day. At Housey in Canteen & then to Anvin. Had some dances in a Cafe. Once more feel quite well.

9 Saturday

Another lovely day. Took it easy in afternoon. Housey in Canteen in evg.

Mem

Now have to go out properly dressed i.e Belt, puttees, swagger stick & G.S. ribbon

10 Sunday

11 Monday

*Fine & <u>very</u> hot. Played Housey in Canteen.
Did not go out of camp.*

12 Tuesday

*Still frightfully hot. Played Housey & then to
Anvins. Feel quite fit. Rations poor again.*

13 Wednesday

*A lovely day. To Maisoncelle in afternoon.
housey in evg & afterwards to ?Codlers shop for
Pontoon. To bed about 12.*

14 Thursday

*Another very hot day. Housey in evg. Rations
still poor. Again saw Demob Officer. No hopes
of getting away yet.*

15 Friday

*Still fine & hot. To a dance in Anvin. Awfully
funny. Very crowded. <u>Two</u> bandsmen. It was*

kept up late. Did not get home until 4.a.m.

16 Saturday

A lovely day again. A nap in the afternoon. housey in evg & then to Anvins. Danced in first cafe on left, tunic off.

17 Sunday

Overcast morn, lovely day afterwards. Did not go out of Camp. Housey & Naps in evg.

18 Monday

Another beautiful day. Adjt informed us that Derby men who joined up before 1/7/16 would be demobbed in their turn!!

19 Tuesday

Still very fine. In evg Housey & Naps. No luck at either for some days.

20 Wednesday

A lovely day. To farm in afternoon. Housey & Nap in evg.

21 Thursday

Heavy rains in night. Another fine day. To Blangy in evg with Wydenbachs. Home about midnight.

22 Friday

Fine, hot & breezy. Housey & Nap in evg.

23 Saturday

Still fine. Took it easy in afternoon. To Concert in evg. (fair) & then to Anvin

24 Sunday

Only a little bread for tea. I managed to secure a quarter of a slice. Many men were unlucky. French bread for breakfast & tea on Mond. Not so fine, some showers during day. In afternoon to Teneur with Vaughan. Housey & Nap in evg

25 Monday

*Not so fine, overcast & some showers. Housey
& nap in evg. asked whether I would like to
stop on at C.W.*

26 Tuesday

Weather unsettled. Housey & nap in evg.

27 Wednesday

*Weather unsettled but fairly fine. Heard from
E that she is crossing tomorrow. To Boulogne.
Arrived about 10. Put up at Hotel near Quay.*

28 Thursday

*Overcast & showery. Explored town in morn.
Met E. about 2 o'c. Shewed her around the
Town. Stayed at Gourmet's Hotel. Went to bed
about 10.*

29 Friday

*Finer today. Had another walk around the
Town & caught 12:30 train to Etaples. Had
lunch at Hotel opposite the stn & left by 3:15
for Blangy. Arrived at F about 5:30.*

30 Saturday

Overcast & close. To Camp in afternoon for part of kit. In evg a walk round Teneur with E. & afterwards to Camp for more kit.

Mem

Drew my rations today (Sat) & not a bad lot either. Received much more than I expected.

~~£22:10:0~~   ~~£18:13:0~~

31 Sunday

Overcast & close. Went for a walk around Teneur after dinner. Stayed in part of evg & then to Camp for rest of kit.

1 Monday

A finer day. To Ranns place for tea. Went with Able to fix up his digs & also to Canteen.

2 Tuesday

A lovely day. Had about a two hours walk with E in evg. Called at Ranns place & also Camp

3 Wednesday

Weather not so fine, some showers. To Azincourt in afternoon with Mr & Mrs R. Tea in Cafe. Home about 9.

£12:18:8

4 Thursday

Finer today. Did some odd jobs after tea & then for a short walk with E. Home about 9.

5 Friday

A fine day. After tea with E towards Teneur & then called upon R's. Later went to C.W. for Cabinet with Ted.

6 Saturday

A fine day. "Tubbed" E in afternoon. after tea E & I went to Anvins. Left E at Rs & I went to Camp, & called for her on way home.

Mem

Men now leave off work at 4 o'c. There is absolutely nothing doing in the Works.

7 Sunday

A perfect day. To Hesdin with Rs. Home about 5:30. Rs to tea with us. All of us had a stroll in evg & then Ted & I went to the Camp & after to Luycettes.

8 Monday

A beautiful hot day. In evg with E to Tilly Capelle ridge through Woods & home via Ration ?Dump & Stores Camp.

9 Tuesday

Another very hot day. A short walk with E in evg. Left her near Stores Camp & I went to Canteen. Home about 9.

10 Wednesday

Very fine & hot again. E & I had a sleep in the afternoon. In evg for a long walk towards Bergenoise, Lovely sun set & full moon.

11 Thursday

Still very hot & fine. After tea with E for a walk pass the old mill & then onto Mrs R's house. Went to Canteen with Ted.

*12 Friday

Very hot indeed. After tea spent some time in garden with E & then I went up to <u>Stores</u> Canteen.

13 Saturday

Still very hot & close. A little rain. For a short walk with E in evg. Nap in afternoon. Both feel a little off colour.

Mem

*Have killed a pig at our house. Baked potatoes & chop for breakfast.

14 Sunday

*Not so fine very close some rain & thunder.
Took it easy in the morn. To tea with Rs &
then to Blangy to see their cousin off.*

15 Monday

*Much cooler: overcast. After tea with E to An-
vin. Called at Stn Cafe. I went into Canteen
on way back.*

16 Tuesday

*A finer day. In evg with E to Teneur & by Old
Mill to Rs house then with Ted to Canteen.*

17 Wednesday

*A lovely day again. In afternoon with Rs to
Auchy by train. Walked back, A lovely walk.
Home about 9:30.*

18 Thursday

*A cool misty morn. A lovely day afterwards.
Out for tea with E. Called on Rs. Ted & I went
to Canteen.*

19 Friday

Overcast chilly & some showers. To Rs with E after tea. Ted & I to Camp for our passes* etc

20 Saturday

A lovely day. E. Mrs R & I by 10:15 from Blangy to Berck. Arrvd about 2 .Ted joined us in evg. Had a good time.

Mem

*As usual found pass unsigned. Called on the Adj in the village & got it signed

21 Sunday

Not so fine-chilly. Left Berck about 11. Reached home 5:30. Had a good weekend. Mr & Mrs Rs to tea.

22 Monday

Overcast & chilly. After tea with E toward Teneur. Not very pleasant walking. Both in very good health & spirits.

23 Tuesday

Dull & chilly. For short walk in evg. met Rs. To Canteen with Ted

24 Wednesday

Morn & afternoon fine bright & windy. Evg overcast. Mr & Mrs Rs& As to Azincourt with us

25 Thursday

Warm but dull. To Rs in evg. "Ran" two cabinets. Major on the war path. Have to get to Office earlier

26 Friday

Overcast & chilly. As to tea. In evg. Neville & I went to Camp & E home with Mrs A. I called for her later. Some ???

27 Saturday

Dull & cold. Warmer in afternoon. To Paris Plage by 10:15 from Blangy. Home about 6. Had a good outing. To Camp in evg.

Mem

Was told on 25th that I must be demobbed to-morrow unless I signed on for a month. Signed form dated 20/9/19 to stay until 20/10/19.

28 Sunday

To Arras with Rs & As. Started raining as soon as we had finished lunch & did not leave off. Spent afternoon in Cafe. Arrvd Anvin 7:20. To Rs to tea.

29 Monday

A lovely day. A walk with E after tea.

30 Tuesday

Hard white frost in night. Fine bright day but cold in morn. Walk with E after tea, called on Rs

1 Wednesday

Bright & warm. Heavy rain & lightening in evg. E & I had nap in afternoon. E did not go out in evg. I went to Stores Camp

£19:0:0

2 Thursday

Very heavy rain during night, heavy showers & bright intervals during the day. For walk with E. To Canteen with R.

3 Friday

Fine & bright. After tea with E to Rs. Went to Camp with Ted to make up pay rolls & then "ran" a stove.

4 Saturday

Dull but warm. To Etaples with E to see grave. Had a pleasant day. Home about 5:30 ~~did not go out afterwards~~ To Camp in evg

5 Sunday

Changed from S time to W.

A fine day,dull at first,brighter in afternoon. To Arras again with E. went out on to Cambrai Rd. Home 8:30

6 Monday

A beautiful warm day. E met me as usual in afternoon & we picked some mushrooms. After tea we had a short walk.

7 Tuesday

A fine day. Short walk with E after tea. Lovely moon. I went to Stores Camp afterwards.

8 Wednesday

A lovely day. Had a nap in afternoon. In evg sat by fire & afterwards I went up to Camp.

9 Thursday

Dull chilly & showery. Sat by fire in evg. Afterwards I went up to Camp for a short time.

10 Friday

A fine bright day E in afternoon to Anvins with Mrs A. We went there to tea. In evg to camp with Neville.

11 Saturday

A fine day. Mushrooming in afternoon with E. To Camp Concert in evg with As. Rather a good show

Mem

Several Officers & men one afternoon went mushrooming in a four seater car?

"C" 12 Sunday

A fine day. Showed E round Tank Park in morn. Packed luggage in afternoon & then to Rs for tea. As there. Had a very pleasant evg.

13 Monday

A fine day, but cold & windy towards evg. Left Madames with E about 9:30 for Boulogne. E left by 5 o'c boat for Ldn. Had a walk round to bed about 10

14 Tuesday

Fine & bright in morn & afternoon. Left B 12:30. Arrvd Madames about 5:30. In evg. went to Camp & returned to Tilly Capelle to sleep.

15 Wednesday

Fine & bright until the evg, then very heavy rain. Had dinner at Camp (stew & rice). Moved kit to Camp during afternoon. Slept in Camp.

16 Thursday

Dull, cold & showery. Stayed in Camp until about 8 o'c & then went for a short walk.

17 Friday

Hard frost in night. Beautiful bright day. Played Housey & then to Anvin with Bill Vaughan

18 Saturday

A nice bright day. Watched football match in afternoon & afterwards went to As for tea & then joined Rs at Concert.

Mem

Rly engine & truck brought men to see football match!!

19 Sunday

A beautiful bright warm day. Played cards in morn & then after dinner to Bermicourt with Titmus, Bingham & Jackson. Picked a lot of mushrooms & had them with pork & potatoes. Had a jolly good feed & outing.

20 Monday

Another fine day. In evg to Farm for washing & to say good bye, & then to Amys. Home early

21 Tuesday

Left Camp about 8:30 by lorry for Blangy. Arrvd Column Camp about 2p.m. In evg went into Town with Jock West.

22 Wednesday

Sat on grass & played cards in morn. After dinner left for Marlborough Camp. Down Town in evg.

23 Thursday

No water in Camp. Went for another wash in brook in fields & then had a walk until dinner time. Played House in afternoon on own.

Town again with Jock

24 Friday

For Blighty!! Reveille 3 o'c. Boat left at 8. Arrvd C.P. at 6. Home about 11. Tired out.

25 Saturday

Not so fine. Up about 11 o'c. To Es in evg. Home about 11 with E. In civvies again.

Mem

Bright & warm from time I left C.W until Frid. evg when it started to rain .

26 Sunday

Mrs Barnard

27 Monday

Meet Harry at Monument Stn at 12:30

28 Tuesday

Meet Mrs R & A at Vic. at 2 o'c

2 Sunday

To Mays

5 Wednesday

Cr £13:13:6

10 Monday

Cr 8:13:6

14 Friday

Cr 3:13:6

18 Tuesday

Moved to 13 Derwent Rd

20 Thursday

Cr 22:13 :6

22 Saturday

Cr 17:13:6

NOVEMBER   1919

23 Sunday

Cr   *11:6:10*

           Shares   *6:5:0*

                      5:1:10

Cr   *15:0:0*

           20:1:10

Cr Shares   *6:5:10*

                   26:6:10

25 Thursday

Had four days holiday. To Mrs E's for Xmas Day & spent the remainder of the time at 62 Mar. Had a bad cold & did not feel well over the holidays

Places Named in Diary

France

Maresquel	Maresquel-Ecquemicourt
Blangy	Blangy sur Ternoise
	Nanny & Grandad lived here
	August to October 1919
T. Capelle	Tilly-Capelle
Erin	Location of Tank Corps
	Central Workshops, 2.5 miles
	north of the Heavy Branch
	HQ at Bermicourt.
	Grandad based here.
	Just Central Stores here from
	29/3/18
Bealencourt	Béalencourt
Abercourt	Ambricourt
Abricourt	Ambricourt
Maisoncelle	Location of an aerodrome in
	WW1
Anvins	Anvin
Bergonoise	Bergueneuse
Hesdin	

Bapaume	Strategically important city in Battle of Somme and 1st & 2nd Battle of Bapaume, 1918
Monchy Caioux	Monchy-Cayeux
Wavrans	Wavrans-sur-Ternoise
St Pol	Saint-Pol-sur-Ternoise The soldier in Tomb of the Unknown Warrior selected from here.
Arras	Scene of many battles in WWI. ¾ of the city had to be rebuilt after.
Anzin	Anzin-St-Aubin All but destroyed in WW1 as base for soldiers & military.
Courcelette	Major tactical objective in Battle of Somme. Village razed & captured by Canadian Corps.
Amiens	Fiercely fought over & occupied, by both sides in WW1. Heavily damaged.
Albert	Key location in Battle of the Somme. Known for Leaning Virgin on Basilica. Town completely reconstructed after WW1.

Auchy	Auchy-lès-Hesdin
Fruges	
Verchon	Verchin
Heuchin	
Teneur	Location of workshops for Tank Corps to repair tanks, from October 1917 one mile east of Erin
Aberville	Abbeville. Never occupied By German troops in WW1. Site of a military hospital during Battle of the Somme. Town partially destroyed
Crepy	Crépy
Montroix	Montreuil-sur-Mer: HQ of British Army in France from March 1916 to April 1919
Azincourt	Named after Battle of Agincourt of 1415
Bermicourt	Location of Tank Corps HQ at Chateau de Bermicourt
St Omar	Saint Omer: HQ for British Royal Flying Corps from October 1914
Etaples	Etaples-sur-Mer: Principal depot &

transit camp for British
Expeditionary Force
Location of Military hospitals
& Military Cemetery, the
largest CWGC one in France.
Town awarded Croix de
Guerre in 1920

Berck Plage	Berck-Plage
B.P.	Berck-Plage
Paris Plage	Le Touquet-Paris-Plage
B	Boulogne
Calais	

*Postcard showing the village of Blangy-sur-Ternoise;
used as a base by Tank Corps during WWI*

GERMANY

Cologne	Target of several minor air raids in WW1, but suffered no significant damage & was occupied by the British Army of the Rhine until 1926.
Coln	Cologne
Orverath	Overath Located approx. 15miles east of Cologne.
Bohn	Bonn: On the Rhine,15 miles south southeast of Cologne
Andernash	Andernach: Town on left bank of the Rhine

ENGLAND

Folkestone	
Vic	Victoria Train Station
L.Corner Hse	Lyons Corner House: Large Art Deco style Tea shops with food hall, hair salons, phone booths & theatre booking agencies

"62"	62 Marmora Road, East Dulwich, SE22. Family home of Grandad. Both his parents still living there in 1919
Pad	Paddington Train Station
Torquay	Seaside town in Devon where Nanny & Grandad honeymooned.
Babbacombe	Beach/town near Torquay
Ansty Cove	Anstey Cove: Small, pretty cove between Torquay & Babbacombe
Daddy Holes	Daddyhole Cove, Near Torquay
Plymouth	
Paignton	
Y.M	??? YMCA
C P	????Crystal Palace
Derwent Road	?????? Nanny & Grandad moved here November 18th 1919

∾

FOOD

Bully	Bully Beef, Corned Beef, tinned. Main staple in the trenches too.
Machoniche	Maconochie: Tinned meat & vegetables: "finest beef", potatoes, haricot beans, carrots & onions. But more often turnips, carrots & in a thin gravy. Not popular!
Rasin Duff	Figgy Duff (Pudding): Traditional bag pudding from Newfoundland, with raisins.

ACTIVITIES

Housey	Possibly Bingo type game.
Nap	Napoleon: Trick taking card game
Pontoon	Card game

USEFUL INFO.

Dode	Grandad's brother, Clarence Carpenter 2nd Lt Royal Fusiliers KIA 17th February, 1917 at Boom Ravine. Buried Regina Trench Cemetery, Grandcourt

E	Elsie. Nanny!
C & V	Cecil & Vera. Grandad's brother, never served in WW1 as reserved occupation (Bank). Married Vera 1921
Mrs E	Mary Ann Egan: Nanny's mother
Mays	?
PC	?
Adjt	Adjutant: Army officer who assists a more senior officer.
M	Married. As mentioned 30th May, 1919: "M at 10.30" !!!!!!!!!!!!!!!!!!!

The photo mentioned on 6th June, 1919 was taken at Dinham & Sons, 34 Union Street, Torquay: a famous photographic business established in 1890s. The elegant studios were frequented by hundreds of distinguished clients.

Waacs	Women's Army Auxillary Corps

CENTRAL WORKSHOP HUTS, OTHER CAMPS ETC

Erin:

Camouflage Hanger

C.	canteen
Supper Hut	
Works	Workshops Moved to Teneur 29th March, 1918
C.C	
Stores	Central Stores-took over all the buildings at Erin after works moved to Teneur
Coblers Hut	??Cobblers or Codlers Hut
3rd Advcd Wks	
ASC	Army Service Corps, at Auchy

Postcard showing tanks being dismantled at the Central Workshops, Erin, France

Other Camps Visited

F Batts Camp F	Battalion, redesignated as 6th Battalion of the Tank Corps in January 1918 at Blangy
Rest Camp	Near Arras
Canadian Camp	Near Courcelette
Rest Camp	Amiens
Driving Camp	St Pol
Com Trench	Communication trench. Dug at an angle to those facing enemy. Used to transport men, equipment & food supplies. Anzin near Arras
Leave Club	British Empire Leave Club, Cologne. Similar to British Army & Navy Leave Club in Paris. Opened as a *"Corner of Blighty"* with everything given free of charge for servicemen on leave.
Rest Camp	Calais
Column Camp	
Marlborough Camp	
F Camp	?Fruges Camp.

VEHICLES

Ford Box
Foden

Lorry
Truck: Family business
of Ben Foden (former
rugby player for
Northampton Saints)
until went out of
business in 1960s

NAMES OF FELLOW SOLDIERS IN TANK CORPS AT CWS

*Burns, W R

Perkins

Barrington

Bradbury

Hinton

Mason, William

*Clark, Joseph W "Joe" *Corbridge*

Masters

Knot

Langley, Tom

Roberts, Joe

Lockley

Jarvis, Willis H *Company QM Sgt*

*Whiteley, William W. "Billy"

*Kent, Thomas *Orkney*

York

Pickup

Barber, Harry

Horner

Madons

Somerville

Clark *Cpl*

*Griffith, Hugh W *Manchester*

Liptrot, Ernest

Thompson

Shaw

Davi(e)s, 'Taffy'

Swift

*Ranns, John Edward *Halifax*

Titmus

Jones

Snow

Garrish, Herbert J

Knot

West, 'Jock'

Vaugh(a)n

Wydenbach, Philip A J

Jackson

Bingham

Peploe, Arthur C R

Noon, Herbert Ernest Walter *2nd Lt*

Fleetwood

Able, William

Passmore, Ernest Arthur

*Garden, James Watsoy *Glasgow*

*Giddings, Thomas Richard *Wantage*

*Miller, G *Leeds*

?Cobler

?Erb

"Ginger" C

Charlie H

Address in diary

My Grandfather and Father c1933

www.ingramcontent.com/pod-product-compliance
Lightning Source LLC
Chambersburg PA
CBHW021134020426
42331CB00005B/763